ELITE DEFENDERS

POLICE FORCES

Geoff Barker

W

FRANKLIN WATTS
LONDON • SYDNEY

Franklin Watts
First published in Great Britain in 2016 by The Watts Publishing Group

Credits

Series Editors: Sarah Eason and Jennifer Sanderson
Series Designers: Paul Myerscough and Simon Borrough

Picture credits: Department of Defense: Spc. Jillian Munyon 39; Dreamstime: 1000 Words 38, Kbiros 17t, Photographerlondon 3, 20, 33, Stefano Tinti 43; Shutterstock: 1000 Words 23, 30, Agolndr 7, Arindambanerjee 1, 4, Bikeriderlondon 15, Chameleonseye 32, P Cruciatti 12, Derek Hatfield 14, Jiri Hera 21, Jbor 24, John Roman Images 10, 37, A Katz 17, Frederic Legrand 34, LukaTDB 9, Marcyano 35, Miamia 19, Monkey Business Images 27, NSC Photography 13, Larry St. Pierre 28, Howard Sayer 5; US Army: Spc Steven K. Young 26; US Navy: Mass Communication Specialist 3rd Class Kristopher Kirsop 41, 45; Wikimedia Commons: Earth 42, Fiatswat800 40, jjron 6, Lance Cpl. Cory D. Polom 22.

Every attempt has been made to clear copyright. Should there be any inadvertent omission please apply to the publisher for rectification.

Dewey number: 363.2
ISBN: 978 1 4451 5039 0

Printed in China

Franklin Watts
An imprint of
Hachette Children's Group
Part of The Watts Publishing Group
Carmelite House
50 Victoria Embankment
London EC4Y 0DZ

An Hachette UK Company
www.hachette.co.uk

www.franklinwatts.co.uk

Contents

CHAPTER 1:
Law and Order

Police officers form a wall with their riot shields at a public protest. They are also armed.

Who is brave enough to stand up against criminals who break the law? Imagine facing a dangerous robber alone and without backup. Police officers find themselves in these kinds of situations all the time. It is their job to maintain law and order on the streets and to keep the peace in communities.

Police officers have three main functions that help to define their work. First, they seek to maintain order: making sure people can carry on their lives normally. Second, they are law enforcement officers, ensuring that no laws are broken. Third, the police serve the general public. These important functions are connected to one another and all are equally important to every member of the police force, from a patrol officer to the chief constable.

Keeping the peace

Always alert

Members of the police force work together in teams to help to keep the peace in our communities. When a crime is committed, police officers take statements from witnesses to investigate what has happened. They may also inform the public about issues and concerns, such as visiting a school to talk about the dangers of drug use. This book will explain the different aspects and roles of the police.

THINK LIKE A LAW ENFORCEMENT OFFICER

Modern law enforcement officers have a difficult job. They have to work shifts, day or night. Officers also need to balance different duties. One day they might be visiting a school, the next they may be acting as mediators, called in to deal with a dangerous argument in a home. Officers must be skilled in dealing with many different people.

A World of Choice

There are many different and interesting roles in the police force. These include being a patrol officer, a motorcycle officer, a detective, a community service aide, a scene of crime officer (SOCO) and an emergency call centre operator. Someone who is good at solving problems might become an intelligence analyst or a detective, while a person with a scientific mind might choose a career in police forensics.

Motorcycles have been used in police forces since the nineteenth century. They offer a safe and fast form of transport for police officers.

Solving cases

Detectives are important police investigators. Their role is to find out information about crimes and to use these facts to work out who committed them. Some detectives oversee teams of police officers who help them to solve particular cases. Murder investigation teams specialise in piecing together evidence to help solve murders.

Intelligence analysts search for information, perhaps using computer records, to help study particular crimes. They might look for links between different cases. They can then recommend ways to stop additional problems happening in the same area.

Woman police constable's hat

THINK LIKE AN EMERGENCY CALL CENTRE OPERATOR

An emergency call centre operator is a frontline specialist who takes calls from the general public and has to keep calm throughout, especially when dealing with a life-threatening incident. He or she must think and act quickly. The operator must follow a script, which includes questions such as: what is your emergency? Where are you? What is your name? Using the answers to these questions, the operator then works out what emergency service is required. Depending on the type of emergency the operator may also ask: are you hurt? If talking to a child, the operator needs to find out the child's age to try to work out what the child should do next.

Crime Scene Investigations

A SOCO may be called out to the place where an incident has occurred, at any time of the day or night. This is how many police investigations start. The SOCO goes quickly to the scene of the crime. The SOCO's first job will be to protect any evidence and he or she will do an initial walkthrough at the crime scene, taking care not to disturb anything.

Finding evidence

SOCOs need to be organised and methodical individuals who work well as part of a team. SOCOs, as the forensic experts present at the scene of a crime, must make sure the team does not overlook any evidence and that whatever is found is not damaged or destroyed. Evidence can include fingerprints, footprints, tyre imprints, fibres, materials, hair and any other biological evidence, such as blood or saliva.

Whether they have an arch, a whorl, a simple loop or a double loop, fingerprints are unique. This is why SOCOs check the crime scene for prints.

Physical evidence might be found at the scene of a crime or on a victim's body. The entire investigation depends on what a SOCO finds, so it is vital that this evidence is protected. The SOCO writes a detailed report about the collection of evidence. Anything found at the crime scene is then taken to the forensic laboratory where it is analysed by technicians such as forensic chemists.

Protecting evidence

THINK LIKE A SOCO

There are three stages of SOCO work: identifying the scene, documenting the scene and collecting any evidence. To do their job, SOCOs often examine unpleasant incidents. They need to prepare themselves to deal with all sorts of distressing sights, including dead bodies at crime scenes. SOCOs must remain calm and professional, making sure they document the scene with care. They will take photographs, sketch the scene, take measurements and document any evidence that is removed from the scene – taking notes about what the item is and its precise location.

TAKE THE TEST!

Could you be a law enforcement officer?

What have you learnt about being a law enforcement officer? Use the information you have read to answer the following questions:

Q1. Name two out of the three main functions of police officers.

Q2. What do murder investigation teams specialise in?

Q3. Who takes emergency calls from the general public?

Q4. What does SOCO stand for?

Q5. What is the first thing a SOCO must do with evidence at a crime scene?

Q6. Name two ways of documenting a crime scene.

Q7. Name two types of evidence that can be found at a crime scene.

ANSWERS

Q1. Any two of the following: maintaining order, enforcing the law and serving the general public

Q2. Solving murders

Q3. Emergency call centre operators

Q4. Scene of crime officer

Q5. Make sure it is protected

Q6. Any two of the following: taking photographs, sketching the scene, taking detailed measurements and taking notes

Q7. There are all sorts of evidence, including fingerprints, footprints, tyre imprints, fibres, materials, hair and other biological evidence such as blood and saliva

CHAPTER 2:
On Patrol

Uniformed police officers have to be alert at all times. They need to be prepared to think and act quickly in an emergency. In this job, events can take place very quickly and the officer must be ready to respond.

A police officer guards a public building during a royal visit in London.

Emergency call!

Patrol officers usually work in pairs to ensure each other's safety and the safety of the community. These officers need to answer all emergency calls from their radio. Every day can provide any number of different situations to deal with, such as traffic violations, fights, thefts and even stabbings.

The officers called to a crime scene are usually those who are nearest to the incident. At the crime scene, they talk to anyone directly involved and they also interview any witnesses. Police officers must listen, take notes and make sure that the neighbourhood is calm once more before they leave to return to the police station. At the station, they fill in paperwork relating to the incident. When that is completed, and if there are no emergencies to respond to, the officers will head back out on patrol.

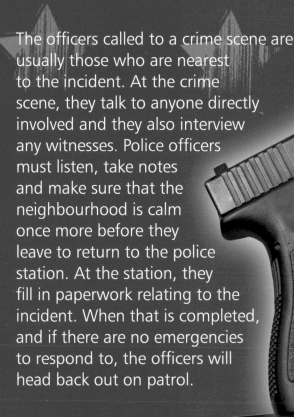

Gun and magazine

THINK LIKE AN ARMED PATROL OFFICER

In some countries, such as Britain, Ireland, Iceland, Norway and New Zealand, police officers are typically unarmed when they are on patrol. In the United States and Australia, however, patrol officers carry firearms. In 2013, the entire Los Angeles Police Department (LAPD) started to use the Smith & Wesson Military & Police (M&P) 9 handgun. In some states of Australia, patrol officers carry Glock 22 pistols. Carrying, and being prepared to use firearms in certain situations, is one of the responsibilities of being an armed patrol officer.

Fighting Crime

In the United Kingdom, during 2014, there were on average around 35,500 burglaries committed each month. There were also on average more than 4,100 robberies (taking the property of another person) each month. Patrol officers have to deal with dangerous criminals, who may be armed. Sometimes, simply patrolling the streets can help to cut the number of incidents.

Burglary

Dangers in the home

If a dispute in a home occurs, officers will often attend the scene in pairs to support each other and deal with the people involved. When they arrive at the scene, they will attempt to calm the situation. They will try to keep people away from the kitchen, where there may be knives. While they deal with the situation, police officers must think of their own safety, as well as that of the people involved.

Domestic disputes require careful handling. Police officers, often working together in pairs, will need to deal with emotional people.

THINK LIKE A PATROL OFFICER

Whether dealing with a domestic dispute or a property crime, the patrol officer must think quickly. If dealing with a robbery, patrol officers will question the owners of the stolen goods, as well as people in the neighbourhood. They will ask questions such as: what was taken? Did the owners and witnesses notice anyone unusual at that time of day? Are there any known thieves in the area? Do the owners suspect anyone? The police officers will then piece together all the information to work out what happened.

Under Threat

Patrol officers sometimes deal with violent crimes, including murder, robbery and assault (sometimes with a deadly weapon). According to the Office for National Statistics (ONS), in the United Kingdom in 2015 crimes against adults dropped by seven per cent compared with 2014. Similarly, statistics show that violent crime has also decreased in Australia, the United States and New Zealand.

Lethal force

In many countries where it is legal to carry guns, these weapons are the preferred murder weapons. However, in countries such as the United Kingdom, where it is illegal to own or carry a firearm, knives are more commonly used. In the face of violence, patrol officers have extensive training to ensure they respond correctly. They are taught how to speak calmly to an attacker. If this approach fails, officers may have to use force so they learn self-defence techniques. Police officers need to know how to disarm an attacker and make weapons safe quickly. Unarmed officers may carry a Taser. This weapon fires barbs attached by wires to batteries and causes temporary paralysis.

Taser

A terror attack results in heavily armed police officers, such as this one, patrolling the streets in case of further attacks.

THINK LIKE AN OFFICER UNDER THREAT

Despite excellent training, police officers cannot know exactly how they will act under extreme stress until they are in that position. Levels of stress can continue to build up over time – being a police officer is known to be one of the most stressful professions. Police officers must recognise that they are under stress. They may have trouble concentrating or problems sleeping. Talking to someone often helps. Experts advise that stressed police officers maintain a healthy lifestyle. This includes regular exercise and nutritious food and making time to socialise and relax with family.

TAKE THE TEST!

Could you be a patrol officer?

Are you observant enough to be a patrol officer? Check if you have been paying attention by answering these questions:

Q1. After an incident, which patrol officer is usually called first?

Q2. After an incident, who does a patrol officer interview?

Q3. Name three countries where police officers are unarmed.

Q4. Which handgun do officers in the LAPD use?

Q5. In 2014, on average, how many burglaries were committed each month in the United Kingdom?

Q6. At a domestic dispute, why does the patrol officer try to avoid the kitchen?

Q7. What term is used for the act of shooting to kill?

ANSWERS

Q7. Lethal force

Q6. Because knives are found there

Q5. Around 35,500

Q4. Smith & Wesson Military & Police (M&P)

Q3. Any three of the following: Ireland, Iceland, Norway, New Zealand and Britain

Q2. Anyone directly involved, as well as any witnesses

Q1. The patrol officer nearest to the incident

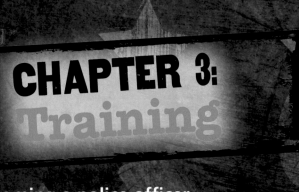

CHAPTER 3:
Training

Becoming a police officer requires intensive training. Officers must know the laws of their country: they must also be trained in first aid and all aspects of health and safety. Trainees learn that police officers need to stay neutral and calm in difficult and dangerous situations.

In countries where officers are armed, weapons training is vital. At the firing range, an instructor gives officers advice on improving their aim.

Physical fitness

Gym work includes learning vital self-defence skills. Recruits also learn how and when it is appropriate to use force. The trainees find out how to subdue a suspect quickly, as well as helping the injured and performing first aid. As part of their training, recruits discover how to be safe around weapons such as knives and guns. Weapons instruction for armed officers starts in the classroom. Trainees learn handgun safety and how officers use a handgun as a 'tool' on the job. They handle firearms standing, kneeling and lying down, and learn to use both their strong and weak hand. Exercises also include firing a gun with obstacles and when lighting conditions are very poor.

Handgun

THINK LIKE A TRAINEE

New recruits seek to impress their teachers and colleagues at police school. Trainees must show they can be both physically and mentally tough, and they can learn a bewildering range of new skills at the same time. Trainees need to pass written and practical tests before they complete their course. Once they have qualified, they can apply for jobs in their local area.

Teamwork

In very competitive situations, it may be a natural response for people to isolate themselves from their fellow trainees. However, it is important for recruits at the police college to get to know their classmates. Training schemes reinforce the importance of teamwork because law enforcement is a team-oriented profession.

If officers work as a team, they can feed off each other's ideas and strengths. In a strong team, each officer will have the confidence to work independently knowing that he or she is part of a greater team. Police departments achieve better results when officers are able to work well together.

Police training stresses the importance of gun safety at all times. Guns should be unloaded when not in use; when loaded, the gun should be pointed in a safe direction.

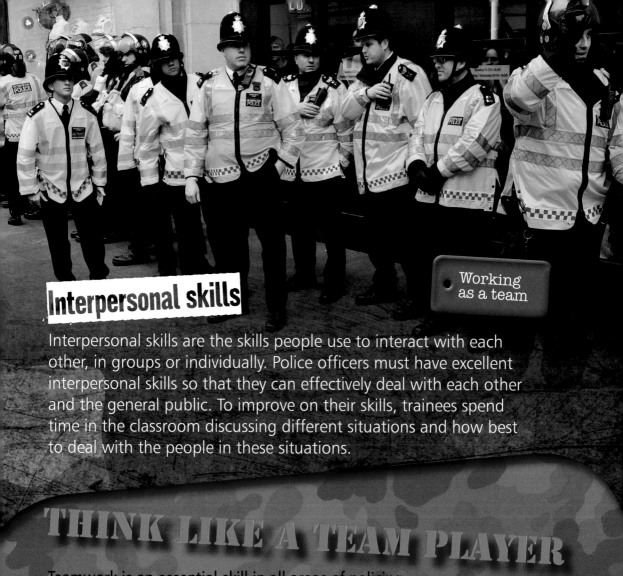

Interpersonal skills

Working as a team

Interpersonal skills are the skills people use to interact with each other, in groups or individually. Police officers must have excellent interpersonal skills so that they can effectively deal with each other and the general public. To improve on their skills, trainees spend time in the classroom discussing different situations and how best to deal with the people in these situations.

THINK LIKE A TEAM PLAYER

Teamwork is an essential skill in all areas of policing. In a murder case, for example, uniformed officers will work together with experienced investigators and skilled forensic technicians. Evidence found at the crime scene is shared with the team to find the identity of an attacker. For example, fingerprints are checked against those held on criminal databases. If there is a match, police officers can investigate further. When different police officers cooperate in this way, the police department is making the best use of its resources to help solve crimes.

TAKE THE TEST!

Could you be a police trainee?

Find out if you have what it takes to join the police force. Use the information you have read so far to answer the following questions:

Q1. Give another name for police school.

Q2. In addition to knowing the laws of their country, what must officers be trained in?

Q3. When police officers are dealing with a difficult situation, they must stay neutral and _____.

Q4. What is it essential for trainees to be when handling weapons?

Q5. With which hand are recruits trained to fire their guns?

Q6. What is one of the main things learnt in the gym?

Q7. What are interpersonal skills?

ANSWERS

Q7. The skills people use to interact with each other, in groups or individually.
Q6. Self-defence skills
Q5. With both their weak and strong hand
Q4. Safe in their use of handling weapons
Q3. Calm
Q2. First aid and health and safety
Q1. Police college

25

CHAPTER 4:
Making the Grade

The methods used to recruit individuals as police officers vary from country to country and even within regions or states in each country. However, most countries and states have similar basic requirements and applicants have to pass a number of tests. The police department will check the applicant's background to make sure he or she is suitable to become a police officer. In addition, candidates will have to pass a physical fitness test and a variety of written, personality and psychological tests.

Trainees have to be fit and they must train hard – even in bad weather.

Physical fitness

In England and Wales, the police fitness test has been standardised so that all officers must pass the same test. The first part of this is an endurance test, which looks at the applicant's heart and lung efficiency. Candidates must run a 15-metre course within a set time, with the time decreasing on each turn. The more turns or laps the officer can do, the higher his or her score is. The second part of the test is a 'push/pull' test in which officers' strength is evaluated. A specially designed device, based on a rowing machine, is used to measure the officer's effort level. The tests taken by Australian officers vary from state to state. For example, in New South Wales, officers must complete the Physical Capacity Test, which tests strength and endurance.

THINK LIKE A NEW RECRUIT

To succeed in their quest to become police officers, young hopefuls will have to demonstrate strength. They will need to show upper-body strength in the demanding physical tests, along with stamina. More than anything, they will need to show perseverance and determination. Police officers must show that they can keep going, even when they are exhausted. This type of attitude can prove that they are mentally strong as well as physically able.

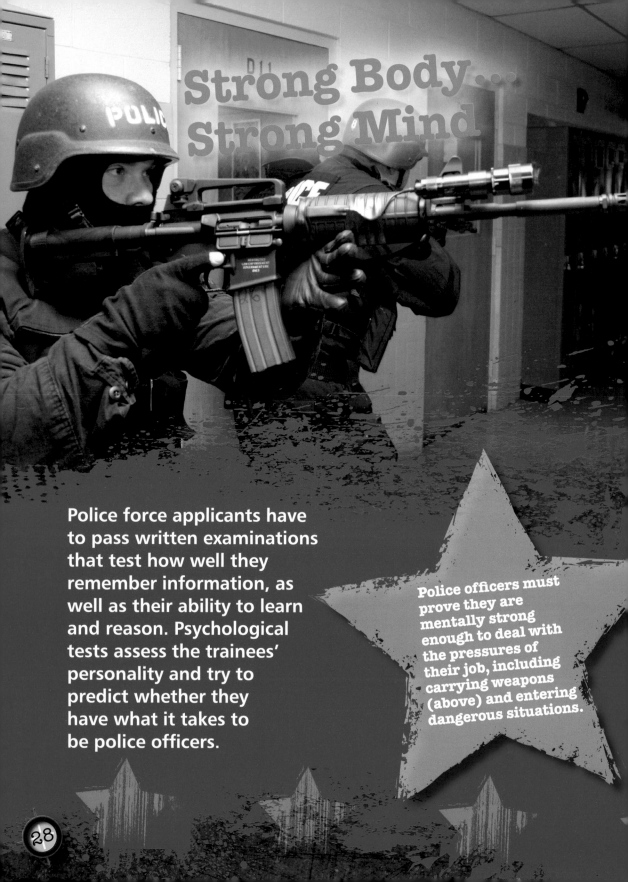

Strong Body...
Strong Mind

Police force applicants have to pass written examinations that test how well they remember information, as well as their ability to learn and reason. Psychological tests assess the trainees' personality and try to predict whether they have what it takes to be police officers.

Police officers must prove they are mentally strong enough to deal with the pressures of their job, including carrying weapons (above) and entering dangerous situations.

Strengths and weaknesses

Police work is tough – and most people will prove not to be at all suited to it. Typical police psychology tests examine a number of key personality features in candidates. Such tests attempt to find out answers to the following questions: how sociable are you? How friendly and kind are you? How organised are you? How calm are you? How creative/curious are you? While there are no right or wrong answers to these questions, certain types of people will be much better suited to police work than others.

Those who show the right personality traits to become police officers also need to be made aware of their strengths and weaknesses. Knowing and understanding these can mean that recruits can focus on their strengths and lessen the impact of their weaknesses in their everyday police work.

THINK LIKE A LAW ENFORCEMENT OFFICER

In countries such as the United States, as part of their psychological testing, candidates are strapped to a polygraph, or 'lie detector'. Polygraphs measure different body functions and reactions, including breathing, blood pressure and perspiration (sweating). Increases in one or more of these may indicate that a person is lying. The machines are accurate, but not infallible. It is important that candidates give honest answers so that their examiners can build an accurate personality profile. This helps to assess if the candidates are suitable for a career in police work.

TAKE THE TEST!

Could you make the grade?

Find out if you have the mental strength to be a police officer by recalling the information you have read:

Q1. What does the endurance test measure?

Q2. How long is the course in the endurance test?

Q3. What does the push/pull test measure?

Q4. In addition to physical tests, what other tests do trainee's take?

Q5. What do psychological tests assess?

Q6. What is the polygraph examination commonly known as?

Q7. Name three functions that the polygraph measures.

ANSWERS

Q7. Breathing, blood pressure and perspiration
Q6. The lie detector test
Q5. A candidate's personality and whether they have what it takes to become a police officer
Q4. Trainees complete written tests and psychological tests
Q3. Strength
Q2. 15 metres
Q1. The applicant's heart and lung efficiency

CHAPTER 5:
On the Road

When police officers explore a patrol area in their car, they are always on the lookout, either for criminal acts or people who look suspicious. Patrol officers stop cars for traffic violations, such as a driver going through a red traffic light. They may investigate JDLRs, when people or a situation 'just doesn't look right'. If police officers investigate a JDLR, they can check out any information provided by the suspect on a criminal database linked to the police car's computer.

A traffic officer carries out a traffic stop, to detain a vehicle in order to check out a possible violation.

Crash scenes

Crash scenes can be particularly difficult to deal with, especially when there are fatalities. Calls to accident scenes require a quick and organised response from police officers. If police officers arrive first at the scene of the crash, officers need to keep calm and work quickly and effectively to make sure that traffic is diverted away from the accident. Often, they will use their own cars as shields to protect the area from other traffic. This will give the patrol officers the chance to check on the injured. Officers need to make quick decisions about injured people and how best to treat them. They may need to give first aid or, if necessary, ask for help from other emergency services, such as paramedics and firefighters.

Radioing for help

THINK LIKE A TRAFFIC ENFORCEMENT OFFICER

At the scene of a crash, officers seek to find out if one driver has caused the accident. They also need to establish if the law was broken, for example, had one party been drinking alcohol or using their mobile phone while driving? Any witnesses to a car crash need to be interviewed.

Traffic Officers

It is the job of every traffic police officer to make sure that drivers obey traffic laws, such as speed limits. Traffic regulations, enforced by motorway patrols, help to improve safety on the road. This is not the only job that traffic officers do, however. They have many other duties. Traffic police report damage to the motorways, for example, after extreme weather conditions. They also have to deal with serious accidents on the road.

Road safety

Traffic police need to have a very clear focus at all times. They must carefully monitor what happens on the roads and motorways in their region, quickly deal with any issues and keep people safe. Safety is the number one priority for traffic officers. Both their own safety and the safety of other road users always have to be uppermost in their mind.

Traffic officers use sophisticated equipment. They can point a radar gun (left) at a speeding car to see how fast it is travelling.

In pursuit

Traffic officers need to know how to control their motorbikes and cars at high speeds. They may have to drive fast on the motorways to catch law breakers. A high-speed police chase in a film may seem incredibly exciting, but in reality, police chases involve enormous skill and officers will always be mindful of safe driving and other road users.

THINK LIKE A TRAFFIC OFFICER

Sometimes, traffic police officers go into schools to educate young people about jobs in the police force. They always take care to impress upon students the importance of safe driving as part of their role.

TAKE THE TEST!

Could you be a traffic officer?

Traffic officers need to be observant. Did you pay enough attention to answer these questions correctly?

Q1. What does JDLR stand for?

Q2. What can traffic officers use to see how fast a speeding car is going?

Q3. What should an officer do with police cars at an accident?

Q4. When dealing with injured people, which other emergency services should a police officer work with?

Q5. Of what medical use can a police officer be at an accident?

Q6. What sort of traffic laws must drivers obey?

Q7. If traffic police drive fast, what is the number one priority?

ANSWERS

Q7. Safety

Q6. Speed limits, traffic lights and not driving under the influence of alcohol or while using a mobile phone

Q5. Give first aid if necessary and if no paramedics are present

Q4. Firefighters and paramedics

Q3. Use them as a shield to protect the crash scene

Q2. Radar guns

Q1. Just doesn't look right

CHAPTER 6:
Militarised Police

Tactical teams can be found all over the world in riot police forces. Such teams sometimes have to face extreme dangers. They are heavily armed and may protect themselves with shields, as well as armoured clothing. Responding to violent situations on the streets or confronting gangs holed up in buildings, riot police call-outs can occasionally end in fatal gun battles. Since the 9/11 terrorist attacks, the threat of terrorism has increased around the world and riot police need to be able to respond.

Thai police commandos

Into action

Carrying arms and ammunition and wearing army-type uniforms, modern riot police officers can look like soldiers. They often wear helmets, fire-retardant balaclavas and ballistic vests. The weapons they carry include submachine guns, carbines, rifles and shotguns, including pump-action firearms. Other tactical weapons that they use may include tear gas grenades, which produce a choking smoke that irritates the eyes, and stun grenades, which create a loud noise and blinding light. While good training and equipment is vital, it is most important that heavily armed riot police officers are mentally prepared for action. They will need to be in a heightened state of readiness.

In Mosul, Iraq, a US Army sergeant teaches Iraqi police how to deal with riots: always face a hostile crowd.

THINK LIKE THE RIOT POLICE

The Special Air Service (SAS), the United Kingdom's special forces unit, started using stun grenades in the 1970s. Since then, many militarised police forces have continued to use these grenades in raids. The aim of the 'flash-bang' technique is to create a blinding light and 160 decibels of noise or more. The unexpected bright light and loud bang will disorientate or stun an enemy for a few vital seconds, giving the police officers an advantage and the ability to disarm the enemy.

SWAT Teams

Special Weapons and Tactics (SWAT) teams are specialist police that wear armoured clothing and carry a range of firepower. In 1964, the United States' Philadelphia Police Department set up the first SWAT team, boasting a 100-man squad to combat an increase in bank robberies in the city. London's SWAT unit is SCO19 Specialist Firearms Command. There are about 550 highly trained officers in this unit.

The presence and number of militarised police officers is controversial. Some people are unhappy that officers, dressed and armed like combat troops, act more like soldiers than police officers.

Dealing with danger

SWAT teams have to face serious riots and crime. In many cities, powerful drug lords fight among themselves to protect their territories. Terrorism is also an ever-present danger today. When there is a terrorist attack, the police force must mobilise a large SWAT team with speed and efficiency. Occasionally, they also have to deal with tricky hostage situations. At these times, it is critical that the police make quick and effective decisions.

Based in Illinois, USA, SWAT K9 is part of a larger team of about 50 officers, forming SWAT FIAT (Felony Investigative Assistance Team). This police response group uses dogs.

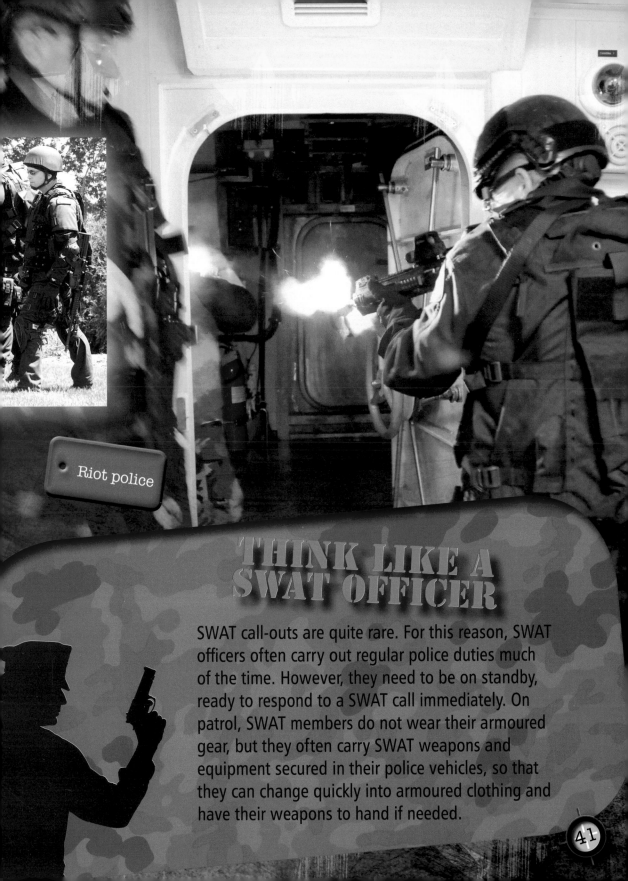

Riot police

THINK LIKE A SWAT OFFICER

SWAT call-outs are quite rare. For this reason, SWAT officers often carry out regular police duties much of the time. However, they need to be on standby, ready to respond to a SWAT call immediately. On patrol, SWAT members do not wear their armoured gear, but they often carry SWAT weapons and equipment secured in their police vehicles, so that they can change quickly into armoured clothing and have their weapons to hand if needed.

Militarised Police Around the World

Around the world, from Italy to India and Malaysia, most countries have their own militarised police forces. One of the most famous of these is Italy's Carabinieri. This militarised police force is older than the country of Italy itself. It was founded more than 200 years ago as the police force of the Kingdom of Sardinia.

In New South Wales, Australia, the riot police are known as the Public Order and Riot Squad. In Victoria, the squad is called the Public Order Response Team. Both squads are heavily armed and their officers are highly trained.

Federal Reserve Unit

Formed almost two years before the country achieved independence in 1957, Malaysia's Federal Reserve Unit (FRU) is a force under the control of the Royal Malaysia Police. The FRU is used chiefly for riot control and other public disorders, but the unit also helps with disaster relief, such as floods.

Malaysia's FRU

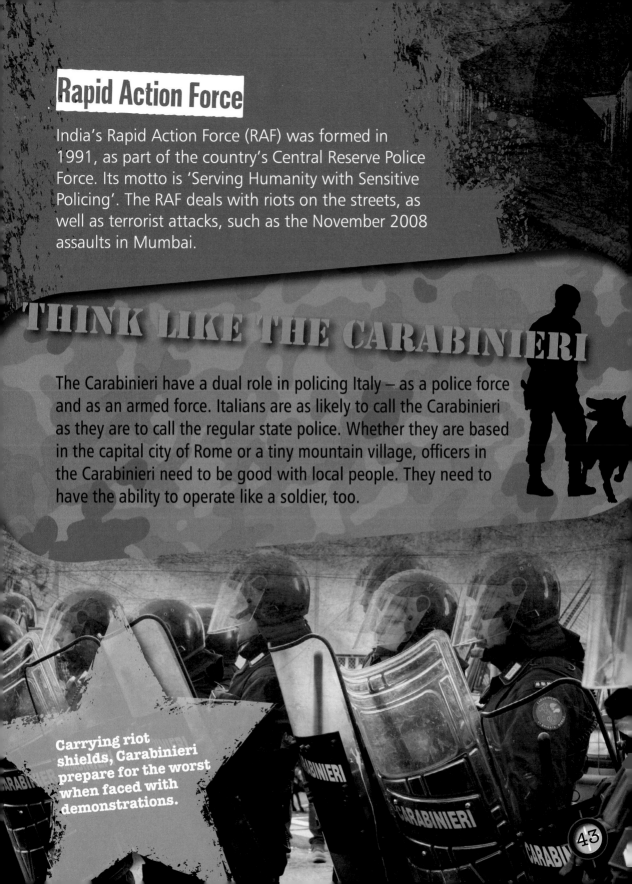

Rapid Action Force

India's Rapid Action Force (RAF) was formed in 1991, as part of the country's Central Reserve Police Force. Its motto is 'Serving Humanity with Sensitive Policing'. The RAF deals with riots on the streets, as well as terrorist attacks, such as the November 2008 assaults in Mumbai.

THINK LIKE THE CARABINIERI

The Carabinieri have a dual role in policing Italy – as a police force and as an armed force. Italians are as likely to call the Carabinieri as they are to call the regular state police. Whether they are based in the capital city of Rome or a tiny mountain village, officers in the Carabinieri need to be good with local people. They need to have the ability to operate like a soldier, too.

Carrying riot shields, Carabinieri prepare for the worst when faced with demonstrations.

Have You Got What it Takes?

Do you want to become a police officer?
Following these steps will help you to reach your goal.

School

Join teams because teamwork is important for a police officer. Work hard and get good results so you can go to university.

Keep fit

Play sports at school. Exercise regularly because police officers have to be fit. Playing team sports also shows that you can work as a member of a team.

Police college

Most police officers attend some sort of police college, where they take physical and written exams to complete their training before they can enter the police force.

College

Completing a degree in criminal justice, law enforcement or a related subject can help you to find work as a police officer. While not required by many police departments, applicants may find a degree helps them to find work in the police force.

Behaviour

You must have a history of lawful conduct so that you will pass a background check. Your past behaviour must show positive features that will support your application to be a police officer.

Work experience

Work experience prepares you for the long hours and rules that come with being a police officer. You do not have to do a job related to law enforcement, although that may help. Work experience shows that you are responsible and capable of doing a job well.

Volunteer

Volunteering with your local police department is a great place to start. However, volunteering with any community service organisation can provide you with some of the skills needed to be a community police officer.

Glossary

ballistic vests body armour that protects the wearer from the impact of bullets

carbines short rifles

combat troops soldiers engaged in fighting

counsellors people trained to give help on personal problems

database a set of information, or data, held on a computer

decibels units used to measure the strength of sound

disorientate to confuse

document to record something (in written, photographic or other form)

domestic relating to or involving someone's home or family

fatalities deaths

fire-retardant balaclavas headgear made of material that does not easily catch fire

forensics scientific techniques used in crime detection

grenade a small bomb that is designed to be thrown by someone or shot from a rifle

homicide murder

hostage a person captured and held by another

infallible incapable of being wrong

intelligence knowledge about a criminal's methods and motives

lethal force deadly force or force used that may result in the death of another person

mobilise to prepare troops for service

paramedics emergency healthcare professionals

polygraph a lie detector test

psychological tests tests that measure mental strength and well-being

recruit a person beginning his or her training

submachine guns magazine-fed automatic guns that are designed to fire pistol cartridges

tactical showing careful planning towards a specific military end

terrorism the use of violence to pursue certain political aims

violated broken the rules

For More Information

Books

Police (Emergency 999), Kathryn Walker, Wayland

Police Officer (Careers That Save Lives) Louise Spilsbury, Franklin Watts

Police Units (Edge – Action Force), Daniel Gilpin, Franklin Watts

The Dog Squad, Vikki Petraitis, Penguin

Websites

This website has links to police forces throughout the United Kingdom:
www.police.uk/forces

This is the official website for Australia's New South Wales police force:
www.police.nsw.gov.au

For more information on New Zealand's police force, log on to this website:
www.police.govt.nz

Note to parents and teachers
Every effort has been made by the Publisher to ensure that these websites contain no inappropriate or offensive material. However, because of the nature of the Internet, it is impossible to guarantee that the contents of these sites will not be altered. We strongly advise that Internet access is supervised by a responsible adult.

Index

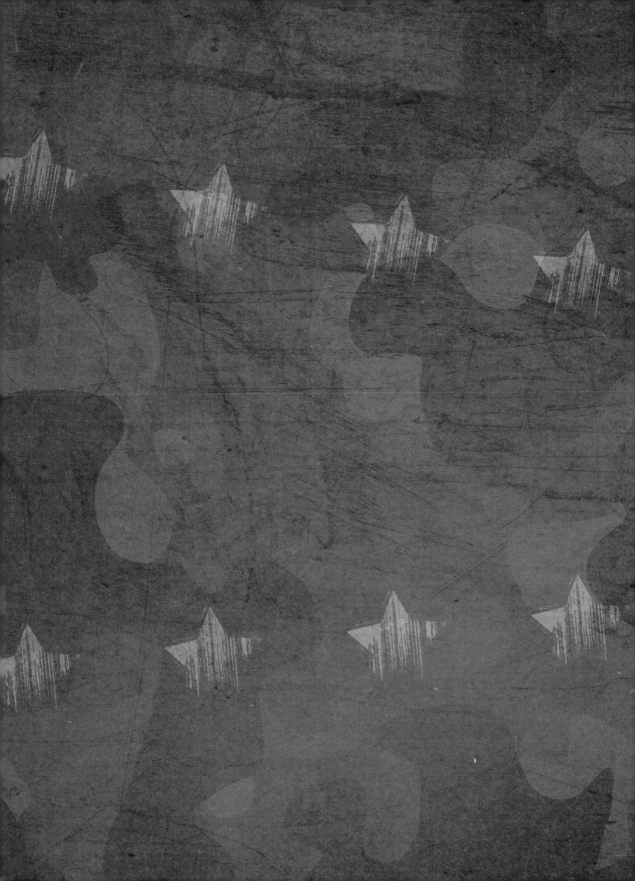